1829

ALISON
BRACKENBURY

CARCANET

First published in 1995 by
Carcanet Press Limited
402-406 Corn Exchange Buildings
Manchester M4 3BY

A CIP catalogue record for this book
is available from the British Library.
ISBN 1 85754 122 7

The publisher acknowledges financial assistance
from the Arts Council of England

Set in 10pt Palatino by Bryan Williamson, Frome
Printed and bound in England by SRP Ltd, Exeter

Funded by
THE
ARTS
COUNCIL
OF ENGLAND

Acknowledgements

Some of these poems have previously appeared in the following publications: *Encounter, The Jacaranda Review, New Writing 3, Numbers, The Orange Dove of Fiji, PN Review, Poetry Book Society Anthology 1991, Poetry Durham, Poetry Review, The Spectator, Stand, The Tewkesbury Admag, Verse.* '1829' was broadcast on BBC Radio 3.

Contents

March Pigeons	9
Brockhampton	10
Gulf	11
Entrenched	12
Tewkesbury	13
The Postscript	15
And the Legend	16
On Wistley Hill	17
Talk	18
Unexpurgated	19
The Queen's Funeral	20
A Winter in Majorca	21
A Chinese Wedding	23
Manchuria	24
Overnight	25
Without	26
Not a Nursery Rhyme	27
The Wardrobe	28
In Bulawayo	29
Near Kariba	30
Odysseus	31
Phil and the Peacock	32
Agenda	33
Going Out	34
Comb Honey	35
Courting	36
Outside the Circle	37
At the Lion Gate	38
Holst Thought	39
Dawn Run	40
The Welsh Cob Show	41
Telling	42
Dealing	43
Asking	44
Hay Fever	45
After the X-Ray	46
After the End	47
Linum	48
Diggers	49
The Boy in Ross	50

Needlehole   51
The Players Come to the Castle   52
Rearing   53
Captain Lord   54
Sub Aqua   55
Your Father   56
Hewlett Road   57
The Spring at Chedworth   58
In the Small Shop   59
Katya   60
'Now we go to the British cemetery'   61
On the Northern Line   62
1829   63
Frost   68

March Pigeons

I have wasted ten years. You did not love me, ever.
You laughed at me, but that was long ago.
When I was far, you thought that I might be
A glittering comfort.

They, the two woodpigeons
Sit on one branch, grow dark with afternoon
Or sun licks round a collar. They are preening
Easy as moulting, heavy, grey and slow.
A curl of white, a single feather, falls.

As boulders wait, these two are beautiful.
I do not envy stones. The ten years are
Heavy as the feather's drifting star.

Brockhampton

The land was too wet for ploughing; yet it is done.
Even the stones of the ridges lie sulky and brown.
The roads are a slide of mud. The wet sky
Is blank as the chink of the hawk's perfect eye.
A blink before the dark comes down
Drops the peregrine sun.

The land glows like an awkward face.
Broken posts, by which sheep graze
Shine pale as growing wood.
Above, the last crow's wings
Cannot frighten from my blood
The stubborn light of things.

Gulf

The grip of frost is hard. The sun is quiet orange
behind the garage trees. Petrol comes in the pump
with a steady knocking, like my blood.
They are driving straight to war.
I do not think they should.
Step back across the concrete, move your head.
The sun goes for your face
in all its savage red.

Entrenched

I drive along the burning road
Where last night's rain and sun blaze high.
False innocence, our element:
No oil is raining from our sky.

In an inside paragraph
A soldier looks back to the spring.
The tanks came first. Then bulldozers
Buried our enemies, still firing.

I do not know their loves or names.
They go, as water into air.
And we are buried, too, alive,
As earth filled up their mouths, their hair.

Tewkesbury

Tewkesbury fields are flat and dim.
They will build houses there, one school.
We come each Sunday, late, to swim

not in the river's brooding cool
(what is the Abbey looking at?)
but in a clean, blue-cloistered pool.

They fought upon the river flats.
There Henry prayed, devout and mad.
God, what are you looking at?

For Richard comes. There is no mouth
to say if he is animal,
a crooked butcher from the North,

or too is trapped by that raw day
would kiss the jewelled cross; would be King.
One shadow trembles in his way.

Child, is it a proper thing
to wonder if he killed with joy
or as the cat's claw hooks, unthinking?

Would it make you wander, weary
outside the light, the looming tower
in waste of fog at Tewkesbury?

Monks bound the small, holed corpse; remember
his praying did not feed another.
The man who stabbed him might rule better.

But voices cry, there were others
beneath the stone of one more tower,
the smothered children, the two brothers.

They swam no rivers, dived no pools.
The Tower's keeper had my name,
held silent, neither saint nor fool.

The mud-breeched armies were the same,
Henry's or York's, the blindest guess.
But afterwards, outside the game

the thick hand finds the bony wrist.
The quiet men come for the key.
They walk towards you from the mist,

you see them now, will always see
though swimming in the tranquil pool
of broadest sun, in Tewkesbury.

The Postscript

(to Mozart's last letter)

'Do what you will with NN. Adieu.'
Was he someone else they owed money to?
'No Name' in Latin, Nomen nescitur?

They flash through the letters, these rich NNs.
They will not lend enough. They elude him again
Though he courts them each day. Then a shadier sense:

'Do not. . . Love, be careful.' Of course they both know
What is happening; or do they? Is this someone who
Pesters in public? Is she going to

Dissolve in the warm spa? Does it, in the end
Stop him from wanting her? Almost a friend
NN has become now, domestic, well-trained –

Why was the other not so tame
Who scrawled through silence when he came
That debt and credit close the same
That loss has every, love, no name?

And the Legend

Who's left, who saw him dance? Old women, holding ever
Backs taut as trees, translucent hands of bone.
They speak beyond you, staring out of daylight –
'When he leapt, he seemed to hang upon the air.'

There are no films; perhaps we should forget him.
Dancers are sneered at, and not helped by him,
The boy passed on from Prince to Polish Count,
To the director's pillow, smudged by dye.
'I hated it. How else could I earn money?'
To leap and flicker, never to be free.

The girl who caught him, on the lazy liner,
Thought he was sleeping late; found him, one day
In a square of sun, naked with sweat,
He worked and sprang, one rail's breadth from the sea.
'Three days after our wedding, when I said
"I must teach you to dance", but she refused
I knew it was no good. What could I do?
White roses, two francs each! Besides, I loved her.'

'Madame,' the brisk Swiss doctor said, 'be brave.
Leave at once and take your child with you.'
(He liked the child; taught her high Russian songs.)
'Some are born mad.' Left stranded on the land
She did not leave him. She would eat red meat.
He pushed his plate away, went missing, sat
Trembling on edges, clung to the whipped birch twigs.
'The tree had saved me.' But to hang on air
Cost the tree nothing, but its patience, but
Cost it nothing. Now we would save trees.
He did not; stumbled, at a walk; did nothing.

They named a racehorse after him. It won
In gleam of neck and cheek, strained, costly flesh.
His hair hung strangely, like a mane, he tried
Nervous, different styles, none ever right.
But speed's a gift, unforced. The name was right,
The swift Nijinsky. He could not stay there,
While those who laugh, eat thick roast beef, are waking.
Miles from land, they tumble tides of air.

On Wistley Hill

Sheep, have you found a shoe?
                                    They were not here
when we rode, boisterous, through afternoon.
They lift their bony faces, strangely white
on the long back of the hill. The reservoir
floats bluer than the sky. A Roman snailshell
gleams white beside the track. The pale farmhouse,
despite the signs for B & B, shines empty.
Grey ponies in the ridge-fields stand unfed.

I wait for the white moon, swollen and eager,
and, meanwhile, I trudge back, to the beechwood
where we slithered over banks. The Thames starts here,
that proud, foul river, in a slime of root.
Oh, day drops and curved twigs mock in their hardness,
my fingers probe the hoofholes, nothing's there,
not owl or badger or the ghostly sheep.

So much, I think, has drowned beneath the wood,
lovers' hairpins, farmers' iron, pigs' bones.
Frightened of rape or loss, I almost run
whistling old tunes, beneath the lightless sky.
How short spring's days are, despite all we do.
Where have the sheep gone? Who will find my shoe?

Talk

Your voice fell rough, to deeper air.
Where has the young high anger gone?
A click cuts hiss of atmosphere.
Upon my solid planet, where storms huddle
I cross the yard, past nettles, buckets, bikes,
To mix the horse's garlic with chopped apples.

Such dampness weighs this summer down
That powdered garlic, fine for coughs,
Has set in pebbles, eggs of brown.
A knife serves up a spray, as blank
As empty stalls. You never showed
Warmth which browns hands, bold gleam of flanks.

Harsh as the garlic's dry, gold flame,
What did you say, unsaid before?
I feed the horse without a word.
The garlic's hot in every pore.

Unexpurgated

Catullus, famous for loving one woman
Who loved too many, I see you did too.
Your poems are tender as skin
Rubbed too often on too many people.
Add on the mess you were in,
Boys, money and parties, no right scheme of things
Could ever have fitted you in.

Only your recklessness breathes,
Our classics are pressed leaves, quite dead.

In the bored courtyard, our autumn,
Hot seed whispers rain on your head.

The Queen's Funeral

Her own horse steps in violet silk.
Black velvet sighs upon her bier.
The Duchess's train is wide as Thames.
The clerks and diarists crowd near.

Later, too late, they find the note
Forbidding all show. As before,
A practical and honest soul,
She'd spend the money on the poor.

Snow whirls on mud. Each coffee shop,
Warm inn stands closed. Her heart's one friend –
Bound by custom, strange in grief –
The ruined King does not attend.

A Winter in Majorca

'Why do we travel?' she writes with a flourish
watching her maid replace books on the shelves
'hope in our hearts – with warmth in our hands –
to settle on that barren land, ourselves.'

They are selling the Majorcan flat. December
strikes white upon arches, the pine-tree sheds
fine hairs on the balcony, where the lizard's small claws shrivel.
Old huts had open windows. Hard rain beat on their beds.

She was not a good writer. But she was brave,
had trunks of books, the young man on her arm.
Glossy-leaved, new oranges entranced their mouths with summer.
Her children teased the dogs on autumn farms.

There we saw castles in the burning noons of Christmas.
My daughter shivered with the flu all night.
The people are reserved, a grey foam licks the beaches.
They fled to Valldemosa. There the light

Like heat out of an oven, on the terrace
Made me flinch; step back into the cell,
With his death mask, the damp unplayed piano.
Nothing in her books could make him well.

She raged against the dull pig-keeping farmers
But slept beneath the fleeces they had cured.
His music pleased; except from that one night,
When she was stranded, with the cart she lured

On flooded roads, with her French money. Rain
Drummed low roofs, his wrecked lungs. Huddled alone,
He knew that she was dead; all her mad schemes
Faded. Christ's blood flickered on the stone

Of the abandoned monastery. He heard
Death hurry down the corridor, pause there,
Drag at his door's handle. There she stood
Shrouded in mud, a river in her hair.

Such fond deceptions in the candlelight!
The stones are slippery; there my daughter fell.
'I do not like this place.' He stroked the fleece,
Sipped her tame goat's warm milk, remembered hell.

Once, as storms cleared, she walked towards the sea.
A girl, met ditching, led them to the place.
She leaned down from the ledge; her tall son dragged her back.
The light struck like a knife across her face.

My daughter now speaks warmly of the island,
Castles and caves, still lit by fever's edge.
Her daughter hated him. They grew apart.
What did she see, hands gripped upon the edge?

No oranges, no soft wool, not his hand
Closed upon the pillow. She was drawn
Into the voiceless whirling of the mist
Whiter than women, fast as the unborn.

Nobody returns to Valldemosa.
She will see much, is strong. She draws once more
On a fresh cigarette; scrawls in hot ash,
Her lie, despair. What do we travel for?

A Chinese Wedding

A Chinese wedding! On the muddy floor
Of the Peach Orchard Restaurant, the guests, in grey
Winter overcoats stood waiting for
'The bride, Mrs Alison. She is coming,' cried our guide
Who alarmed me, with her hunched good coat,
Her husband, the dark editor. Outside
Snake firecrackers woke the streets with smoke.

The bride towered fire-red: the fabled bird
Which rises from the ash; or as the smoke
Faded, in rich skirts, a scared slim girl.
'She works in the station,' Mrs Zhe declared.
Had I seen her, trousers baggy at the knees
In the dingy panelled waiting rooms
Left, still for Soft Class, by the Japanese?

In her rough book I scrawled 'Congratulation,'
Her father filled my hands with fruited sweets.
Would she grow, like Mrs Zhe, a 'dragon lady,'
Lips closed to question in a fair flushed face?
For terror breaks both sides. 'Now you have seen
Our part' (she almost sighed) 'you must go south
To the mountains. Rivers there, I think, are clean.'

Red is old danger's colour: blood on books,
The wrong seed, dead in poor ground, Zhou En-lai
'Who did and spoke against his will, because
To save some, to do good, he must endure.'
The girl's small fingers touched, withdrew. Whose son
Lies lost in dark, hands outstretched to that fire?
It licked her sleeves. It once loved everyone.

Manchuria

Slowly, the man, along the frozen road,
Pedals; breath steams; and half of China gleams.
The brushed trees stand in flickered rows,
White cloths strain tight on each train seat.
Our guide slips in to sell us coins; of course
It is New Year; and on the copper glows
The stiffly trotting figure of a horse.

This young man, of uneasy age
In silver glasses, taut and slim
Speaks slowly of the climate's change,
'The sun is angry,' huddles in
His hood at probing questions. For this year
Borne with scared English south, he burned
To join the students in the square.

Plays on a Chinese stage, I know,
However long, end the same way.
A man appears, unsmiling, old,
The audience is sent away
To the black cold. In their evening
You wander, for you could not join
The crowds in the guns' battering.

So you are 'nervous' as they say
Of those still numbed by the last purge
Who lost their children, choked each day
On rational lies. It flares, the urge
To run from silence on the guns,
The rest are beaten in the gaols.
The young dead were the lucky ones.

Laying the coins on the white cloth
He points to 'seasons', lunar signs.
What is that gleaming character?
'Ah – that means glory,' he replies.
Smiling, he leaves without a word.
I watch a mule-cart draw its load.
Turning, sudden as a bird
The man swoops off the frozen road.

Overnight

This is the Tangshang sleeper where
the chef sits drunk in the dining car

'There is no gas for heaters' so
the air inside is chill as snow.

In Soft Class, wrapped in grubby piles
of blanket fur, we let the miles

Of metal ring our bones and boots,
but cannot sleep, since Chinese flutes

Mourn through the speakers everything
the winter child dreamed, sleep till spring.

This dry land, neither small nor kind
will haunt me when it drops behind

As I sleep, as if dead, until
scuffling wet leaves, the sparrows shrill

Who cannot wake the drunken man
upon the sleeper to Tangshang.

Without

When you were born, the gales began.
First there was the great dry harvest wind
Rattling each window of the corridors.
Then, the hill-storm: where poor grass, bent trees
Swam up to you in rivers of the air.

High in a stone house in a northern town
Without your cries, I am about to sleep.
Something bucks and bangs. It is the pinned
Frame of the old sash which pulls me back,
Waiting, in this stillness, for a wind.

Not a Nursery Rhyme

Is it boring to be a princess?
With smooth hair perfectly brushed
You stare through carriage windows
At a small girl kicking dust.

Your glances meet, through rainbow glass,
Then you think again
How sharp-edged each stone must feel,
And how cold the rain.

The Wardrobe

'I want to be pretty!' 'You can't wear that dress.
You'll be climbing ropes. They have swings in the tree, remember?
You would freeze in such thin sleeves.
The afternoons are chilly in September.'

'I was warm, finding fossils by the horse trough.'
Sun struck my back. I sat upon a stone.
I heard the birds shout endlessly.
I thought of nothing for a long time.

'That was at ten. We won't arrive till three.
There is no way that you can wear that dress.'
I would, also, have kept the day the same,
Held the sun at height, the heron's flight,
Where dress is silence, sky a moving flame.

In Bulawayo

In Bulawayo, my daughter sings 'Hot bird!'
In the sticky nest of the hotel truckle bed
her fingers curl like claws to spell the word.

In the neat aviary the noon sun dapples,
an eagle with a ruined wing wades grass,
watered, as where a child waits under apples.

'We are building a clinic,' our guide says, 'where
women rest after birth.' The crocodile
drifts with his snake's eyes sealed. He does not care

that through black airless night, no rain was heard
on tin roofs, hotel glass. Only the wind
stirred Africa, an eagle, winged. Hot bird.

Near Kariba

In the small plane to Bumi
rattling from runways, I saw
a small table, spread with yellow, stand
in the green of the rain, of tough African grass
by the scrub, by the tarmac, the blue frown of cloud.

It is Livingstone's table, scratched with his sweat
and immaculate lines as he sketches his plan
for coffee plantations in view of the Falls.
The hippo munch glossy sprays, night after night.

It is the camp table where Rhodes sits to meet
with the Matabele, who nod, who make peace.
They are given drains; God; bungalows.
Still the nightjar accuses, a whirling white bat.

It is a table upon the rough lawn
of the house in the deep wood, the tollkeeper's house
where somebody spends out-of-London weekends
where cowparsley drizzles, the elders grow rank.
They have all gone in, but the tablecloth gleams
as a woman's dress flickers, reserved, apart.

All you bring to this table are stained lies: your hands.
Like wings they flash open, stiff valves of the heart.

Odysseus

He went in the new-painted ships.
All his good food quickly left,
rolled in the stomach of those endless dips.

Then there were orchards where they spent
short evenings after fighting, hacked
fruiting branches for the meat they burnt.

With all the apples gone, they also lacked
cattle and water; for the spring had dried.
It was the wildest plan he backed

which broke in the small city; which they burnt.
The princes took the women and the gold.
His ship was splitting. Then he learnt

waves grow no smaller, reeling home.
The girls' damp arms in island beds
clutched round his rib-cage like the murderous foam.

So he came back, with no one at his side,
stood by the gate, a stranger to his parts.
The old dog licked his finger-tips, then died.

He fought with all who lived near her, their hearts
ashes from the years of food and beer.
She missed him deeply. Yet she kept her arts.

Sun sucked the finest blueness of the air.
He gripped her waist. The great bed held its marks,
tides of their work, long sleep. He went nowhere.

Phil and the Peacock

It was not old age; she was always lame,
born in Argentina, to the dazzling dawns,
then polio, which caged her in her limp.
She did not marry. She bought children cards
till she forgot, grown looser in her skin
which yellowed to the colour of the slabs
pinning down the weeds of her small garden.
No one answered in the snows. The dustbin rolled,
the church's letter told us of her death.
Now I forget her, surely, as she was,
her throat in loose folds, like a chrysalis.

It is March. The air is dull, but it grows warmer
as I hurry for my daughter, out of school.
Something thin and black lifts from the pavement,
a crisp leaf, a survivor of the snow.
The bent legs are slow stilts. I pick it up,
thinking it a battered tortoiseshell.
The great wings are unbroken; as I set it
down at her gate the wings dip briefly open.
Blue circles are the peacock's startling eyes.

It has no strength, I'm sure, to walk away.
When I come back, I'll show it to my daughter,
lift it in careful cup to our viburnum
(above the tawny cat she used to call).
We reach the place, beside the steady stone.
There are roots, a blue crisp-packet, no black wings.
It has crawled to safer darkness. Or has flown.

Agenda

It is said, we tell our truths in private,
on crumpled pillows, over the stained cup.
It is in public. At the yawning meeting
the thin man straightened up
spoke, as the gilded china rattled round,
one sentence of an absolute despair –
the biscuits snapped to dust – but not to us:
to one he loved, who lived, and was not there.

Going Out

Nature does not exist. Dissolve him, her, it
into water, air; into a hillock
of rough, dead grass where the winter ponies stand
matted with mud, manes beating in their eyes.
You can see them from the road. If you walk close
they will smell you on the wind. You meet their eyes,
bright as stones on your fingers; more lustrous than your own.

As you walk back, stumbling over molehills
(the moles have left circles and chains of fresh black earth
scarring the field. What does this mean?) you see
a single dandelion. Spinning with green, it pushes
through February's damp air, while the ponies cough
for spring. Next light, the track is rock from frost.

There is waste; more waste. The dandelion's seeds
would have ridden the roads and the valleys of air
fallen on stone, the ponies' blank manes,
fallen on frost. Do not be confused
when thaw softens ruts, when the moles raise again
their unfinished circle, the shotguns blast
light birds from hard air. Nature is an excuse,

spits the gipsies' blaze by the bristling wood,
quickly disturbing the badgers' slow night.
Trespassers upon parcelled land
with old cars, tall children, they build up their fire,
a snapping stream through the raw afternoon.
Washing hangs, tethered, unable to blow.
Where is our summer, the fine heads, the silver
noons of long grass? The sparks fade. The sparks glow.

Comb Honey

It is from New Zealand. It must have come by sea,
only the impatient traveller flies,
not this slow stuff, in the long seal of cells
the blunt knife blurs and frees.
The snows of wax float finely to the teeth.
The ships are filled with honey on the seas.

Courting

In the hurt half light of the street
On the bare lawn, two foxes meet.

The first metallic barking finds
Me shocked from sheets, cricked through the blinds.

The rowans and the flowering bush
Are struck to strangeness by a brush

Which bounds away – the only white
In the drained underseas of night.

The second crouches, by our car.
How desperate their voices are

The yapping laugh that turns to scream
The throat's bark, echoed round a dream,

Pursue them as they slide away
To railway cuttings, brambles. Day

Brings us thin January stars,
Steam's spit, the first, fast growl of cars.

Outside the Circle

I worked through all your tricks. I slit the sleeves,
I tugged fine strings which joined the handkerchiefs.
The disappearing girl was always there
Crammed in compartments false as her dyed hair.
I burned the cards you nicked with hidden signs.

Solid as smoke, the moon walks on the square.
Magician, can you call back half your loves?
Dust, the empty seats await you there,
Light; and the astonished flight of doves.

At the Lion Gate

You have been here. But do you know the story?
The storm clouds pass like sheep above the plain.
From this low hill the tall king Agamemnon
Left for Troy, came carelessly again
With the dark princess, Cassandra. Her long grief
Was to tell truth no living soul believed.

She smelt the blood and froze against the doorpost.
Agamemnon dropped her arm, then strode inside
To his small and smiling wife. Fresh from the bath
Slithering on blood and soap, he died
Hacked by his wife's small hand. No pity's in this stew.
She ran outside, to stab Cassandra too.

Their bodies have all gone. New families
Swarm like bees round these confusing stones.
Oh, and her son killed her, went briefly mad;
With a steadied mind he came alone
Nodded to the lions of gate and years.
The autumn's rain stung in his face like tears.

My daughter swings her scratched legs from a ledge.
'Did she wait here? Then why not run away?'
She was too tired. She pressed against the stone
As the strange ribs bruised hers, saw on the plain
The blue speck of a shepherd whose grandson
Dropped for gold, into that stinking place
Where his bare toes crushed Agamemnon's face.

'You are Cassandra,' cries my daughter, shrill.
The lions say nothing. Do not step inside.
While they are knotted in their private war,
Stand, although stiffly, run and hide.
There is always one thing more
Small streams to dam, a child to save,
Bees mutter, blue in thyme; come back, Cassandra,
Warm from your loveless grave.

Holst Thought

Holst thought, and Hardy,
the hills never change.
You could walk the tough grass,
kick moodily at tussocks, start a lark,
and trust this would not pass.
How deeply they were wrong. The lark insists
the past is the song
of our present only. It persists
high and briefly. The wings tire, volcanoes
pour down these valleys. We can trust
the glint at sight's edges, moving away.
In the sky's country, the cloud mass spills
past a fleck – the lark – into bays of ice,
mountains of night, enduring hills.

Dawn Run

Sunday and so clear a day
That as I drive in rush and strain
I wonder why I cannot rest
To live as easy as the rain.
Fretting under traffic lights
I see a pub sign newly hung,
A glistening picture of a horse
With under it a name. Dawn Run.

She won her race at Cheltenham,
Cleared Gold Cup fences, mile on mile.
The cup her owner waved to us
Blurred mud and strain beneath the smile.
I held her shoe once in my hand,
A broad foot, and a heart to match.
They flew her off to France to win,
But there she fell, and broke her back.

So I remember why it is
I do not pass her brilliant face
To drink and in my ease, forget
The pain that is another place,
That is the cost of any prize.
If we had weighed their price, why then
Who else would taste this perfect day,
How many mares, how many men?

The Welsh Cob Show

This cup of hills unfolds a world of horses.
The children, kicking, moaning, are ignored
or sent back to the lorry with the collies.
Girls in chewed jackets lean across the rails
their eyes not on young men but on the horses.
Old men run with the heavy boots of farmers
baying at stallions, for the deepest bone,
the finest silk at heel will go uncounted
unless the forelegs strike from trot to fly.

My child only likes the swept-up skirt
of the side-saddle lady, who's unplaced;
her crime, no doubt, distracting from the horses.
You most admire the black and gilt of traps
whirling past a stream. Time is confused.
You buy her nothing, me a book of horses.

When my daughter rides her sullen sleep
blank as the mountain sky, and you are, too,
crumpled in bed, I scan through lists of horses.
John Evans and his cob lived on the moor's edge
with walls so thin they heard each other breathe.
He raged if his grey stallion lost. They lived
half a man's life-years, walked the roads of Wales,
serviced mares, dragged carts, ploughed stony ground;
they are not needed now yet still I read
(as I might of my own Welsh grandfathers)
of those who are not blurred by photographs
dated or measured but are simply names,
Black Jack, Flyer, Bess and Satisfaction.
It is too late to read on but I sit
as they did last night, shining wheels and bridles,

as those stout single women who bred ponies
saw a black foal through glasses on the moor
waited two springs then bought back from the round-up
the champion. Like a star's whirl it courses,
high above the ground's swell pulses, blind:
has nothing in this world to do with horses.

Telling

Yes, it is broom. It has long licks of flower
In dark still spikes on the railway bank.
The train snorts and fidgets, till I see the smoulder
The tawny, thorned gorse of the opposite bank.

Between runs the naked live shine of the rail.
You were smoother than gorse; the fine broom is too frail
For my toughened skin. Raw heat streams from the sky;
Why did I want you, or tell you this? Why,

Since the whole earth may burn, there is need, there is room
That I should tell now the gorse from the broom.

Dealing

For you, a card, for you, a smile
For you, a life, for you, much love.
For you, a thousand small washed clothes.
'Of money, time,' I tell the child,
'You have so much; so spend it well.'
'Things should be one!' your fierce voice said,
But things are not. I hear time tear
Like an old sheet that's washed threadbare.
What shall be seen through this jagged door?
Blue sky, bright sky, or the wild
Branches' wind-tossed marvellous space
For you, for night's blaze, for the child?

Asking

A painted cart in the lorries' wake,
was drawn by a skewbald, trotting high.
A hunting greyhound padded loose.
Chickens sat crated, and a child,
fair hair as dense as a bramble bush
swung out bare legs as cars swept by –

so the horse-dealing gipsies came.
I saw them. I am told of them.
All the farm gates have been tied
against the motor caravans,
their tides of rubbish, but with these
the farmer, like a schoolboy, sips
his new-smoked tea beside their fire.

I knew a gipsy once like them:
a one-eyed man named Hezekiah.
He's dead and in another place.
But these have burst with the wet spring,
soon as the swifts came, trawling mud.
Their twenty ponies line the track
by ash and hawthorn. I have longed
to ride there by their ribboned fires;
but fear my horse would swerve away.

They can ride bareback on the roads.
They can make tents of poles and sacks.
If they despair, in storms of rain,
or beat the dog, I do not know.
Their spokesman has, it is agreed,
a strange voice, courteous and low.
The farmer, firm on his own land,
asked 'How do you live like this?'
as of an awkward brother.
'Once you have lived this life,' he said,
'you'll never ask another.'

Hay Fever

For Robyn

Eyes swell, as from a blow; you cry.
I have to fight
To keep your dirty fingers out of eyes
Which almost close
As you stumble past the plumed grass of the lane
The choking elderflower, the painful rose.

What is pollen, anyway? you sniff.
The dusty air
Veined with its passages of gold, as if
You were given presents everywhere.
Summer, for which you longed, to which you raced,
You cannot bear.

After the X-Ray

If he had stayed
in the four white walls
or alone in his patch, the untidy hedge
strewing its roses through empty hours
he would never have met the dark mare
whose neck he licked by the elderflower
whose kick snapped his straight cannonbone.

For sixteen weeks he must stand in the straw
watching the light wash and ebb.
All warmth will have flowed past when he stumbles out
November's wind raw on his leg.
Was it worth it? He shuffles, he cranes to the lane,
calls her, and calls her again.

After the End

I am back in Milan. A small light burns
By the Virgin's broad face. Learning the prayers
Took me a long time. But this is my kingdom.
(He left the broad island.) The tide of noise swells,
The muckcarts, the children, the beggars.
                                           I wake,
Marooned by white dawns, warm and stupid with spells.

Linum

It is not tall enough, it will not make a crop –
it has changed its name. It used to be flax,
maker of sheets for fine ladies' beds.
Now it is linseed; feeds cattle.
It is high as a knee, blown with threads of leaf,
scattered with flower. What corn is blue?
They are mouths, they are stars, they gleam sweet
as those pictures of children under dark leaf
in frames of deep gilt. It knows nothing;
the sky is bitterer. Last night's sun
was icy lemon, with drifts of grey;
the morning's blaze is for storm. The flax flowers
begin to shimmer, with a metal edge,
to reflect ripe cloud, race a colder sea.
The flies still whirl in hot air, and I
rise quick up the ridge, through the brief, starred fields.
It is not every day you can run through the sky.

Diggers

Of course he was dead. Yet he spread so wide,
his digger's hands curled, I went back to see.
No mole could grow more. He was pocket-sized.
His fur was not black. It showed silver sheens
smudged open by a finger, ash and brown.
He had been earth's. He was easy with death,
he rippled, he swam. I could not put him down.

Mining my pocket, he travelled to meet
the child's hands. He flowed over her palms
with white pocked leather on his feet
his pink claws harder than my arms.
In glare of day we do not feel
them working by us, all around,
stop, or think them lovely till
they have slipped underground.

The Boy in Ross

The boy knocks at the door. He cannot see me
In the car park by the birches' shiver
Though his face flashes round.
He knocks and waits.
It is a steep street in a small, old town.
The house is like a butcher's or a mason's
With tall straight windows. One glass only glows,
The light is curious orange, almost warm.
The panelled door shows nothing.
The boy's head leans
On the rough cream stone,
He settles down
In his red coat, against the evening air.
I had forgotten how long children wait.
Someone is there with paperwork half finished
With hills of washing up, not bothering
Like me. He sits there, balanced on his bike.
Then I see a friend is circling round
Restless in the shade; a casual call
On friends or almost friends. They shrug, and fly
Down the hill, as steep as to the sea.

Yet when I saw him he was poised
Perfectly alone,
The high door not a stranger's
But his unreachable home.

Needlehole

The roads are miles from Needlehole.
The house burned down, its pictures' suns
Glowed white, fell ash.
It was mortgaged twice
Then under-insured. The untamed lawns
Run pale and thick to the shadowing wood.

Here you saw a golden bird
Dip and flash at the edge of sight
Brilliant back swallowed up by the wood
Where orchids crowded on treacherous banks.
It was never ploughed. The bogs would drink
Tackle, horse, through the skin of the grass.
You thought the bird rare: an oriole.

The frost clings hard in the sunken gate.
Upon me, from the deep dead grass
It bursts, a smoky yellow back,
Woodpecker, yaffle, blood on his head,
Midwinter's sun, green smudge of wings,
Long glint for a beak. Stray leaves glitter yellow,
Hips flicker red, in the deepening frost.
Its cry dips, invites. I do not follow
Where the colours melt. Nobody could.

The winter stars rise in us.
The oriole calls from the wood.

The Players Come to the Castle

It was a dream of welcome,
After miles of storm
The table steamed with cakes and game
The royal fire sprang warm.

Our leader's lines. Now I, the poor
Boy playing queen, tell what I saw.

The hall lay dark and icy,
Its scarlet rugs rubbed bare.
No word or gesture came from
The prince, slumped in his chair.

Rearing

She once picked one up. Like a tiny buzzing bee,
it hovered in her hand, ticked with yellow and brown,
smeared with the dust and straw of the yard
where, by a spaniel's nose, she found it crouching.
The farmer thanked her. There must be
a hole in one box. The boxes, a brown
tower, stood tottering in the yard
emptied of voices. He left, crouching
under the mesh into the end stable,
where it joined the rush of the others, hundreds
lapped in clean sawdust, warmed by a lamp
in quick whirls of dust and the creak of the door.

What she heard from the neighbouring stable
was a whispering clamour, like bees, in their hundreds,
lifted in skeins and swirls to the lamp.
What were they doing, all day, by their door?

She asked the farm's child, who dipped in to visit,
'Oh,' he frowned, 'the little birds? Running –'
He heard slow boots, his father climbing.
'They try to jump over their water, they fall.'

She listens to them, on her hot day's visit.
'Can they fly?' 'A little.' Brown wings drum, running
the column of light, the first guns, climbing
the sun's fierce chamber. They shiver. They rise.

Captain Lord

Captain Lord is on his sofa when the boy comes rushing down.
'Sir, there are rockets!' 'But what kind are they?'
Nobody mentions the trail of white stars,
distress flares from Titanic, half a mile away.

Nobody mentions. I doze on my sofa
watching the gas crackle blue upon bars.
They are many as leaves. They fall silent, like snow.
They glitter our closed lips, the millions of stars.

Sub Aqua

I ought to ring the man about the diving.
Yes, I have tried; but he is never there.
In what blind depth – I ought to send a note.

Still you keep asking me; I do not think
Your swimming strong enough. Your arms are weak.
No sun can reach down there. You would not float.

Through our dry workshop's door a young man brings
A great bell from a German submarine.
Sea ate the clapper, yet for seventy years
It tolled the drowned, the salt stiff in its throat,
It tolled the dead, with silence for its note.

Your Father

I thought he was dying, the old man
Who had lived through wars, seen streets pulled down
Glass towers rise, the rich remain.
I was watering my garden, in May's heat.
The sun is always best before a fight.
Indoors I set a cross by something which
I thought, in some dry future, I might lose
Which I was then too tense and full to use.

He has not died; true, he has not yet fired a letter
At the papers, but he rang up, hot and better.
He raged to be set free. I have not seen him. But I saw
White water from the pipe pulse up and gleam
By the unpruned, blue-green honeysuckle screen.
It shook to rings. Drops bounded, more and more,
As fireworks shatter: each a glistening stone
The wind poised with the crying of the phone.

Hewlett Road

There is a corner where the shelves of cedar
Lift, marooned in seas of offices.
I saw them from a coach in desperate panic
In useless love I flashed before their shadow.
Driving sedately, with a munching child
My breath still alters at their stormy blackness
And I think too: where does the right road go?
(The coach swung left.) Into a rush of streets?
To miles of racing tarmac, with no stopping?

In the end, you must go everywhere.
Across ten years, inside this little town
I need a car park, so I pass the trees
As through a gate. The streets lean in, grow narrow.
There are arcades, painted but empty cafés,
A crumbling theatre. It joins a street I know.

So now I drive there daily. But it is
Not that road. It has gone somewhere else,
Past a place where people walk with care
From light to shade, beneath the shelves of cedar.

The Spring at Chedworth

There is no goddess in the spring
the sturdy walls are bare.
The painted plaster crumbled
colours danced into the air.
The Victorian explorers
found their nymph no longer there.

She would not wait to greet them
though her mouth was never still.
Her baths, where girls sat idly
they miscalled a fulling mill.
'Nymphaeum' fades their labels
where the empty waters spill.

I have seen her in the August yard,
shriek, beneath the hose,
leap in a Welsh river
in her rough and sweat-streaked clothes.
But desire runs through her fingers
she is gone as water goes.

She left inside her basin
a black beetle which clasps tight
a bead of air, her glistening gift,
as he spirals, out of sight,
as the cuckoo in the wet trees
as her laughter in the night.

In the Small Shop

In the small shop, where apples shrink,
Potatoes sprout, the lettuce is green leather,
Past tins, they draw me, bright enough to drink,

Red pools in the brown crumpled bag. No lip
Curves so fully. Nipples are shabby roses.
A knee might shine as roundly, briefly glimpsed.

Their skin is flecked, as fish in sunlit water
Hang. The bitten flesh is oddly pale
As though unripened. 'Do they,' asks my daughter

'Have pips?' (She hates pips.) 'Only one large stone.'
Which I have seen, sucked yellow and quite bare
On sunlit pavements, which I crossed alone.

Say, if you must, the look of them is best
Tense skin, sour water, then the jar on teeth
From foaming flower to salt wave, better guessed.

The sun is rising slowly past the trees.
The crates and bundles shift upon the deck.
The people stand in silence on the quays

Waiting, leafed in mist, for the first ferries.
They glisten, held in darkness, smoulder. Nothing
In all the world's wide summer tastes like cherries.

Katya

'In old Russia,' says Katya, raising blue eyelids,
'There were no thieves. You would knock on a door,
If you were travelling on pilgrimage,
Then people would open, at all times of day.
They would give you a bed, for God's sake, and your supper –
It is very hard, now, to find somewhere to stay.'

'I have three fridges,' says Katya, 'a big one
In which I have put – do you say? half a cow?
Oh and milk; many things. When the winter has gone
April is dirty. The snows melt and run.
But it is not as cold as when I was a child –
Thirty-eight below zero. Why are you not Christian?'

The rattling train slows. 'No one calls me Katya,
But my close friends, my mother, and so.
Ykaterina Vladimirovna!'
She chants to the rails. At their trancing pace
Boris, in charge, pads the corridors
With his long cigarette, his creased, brown, anxious face.

Her silver cross glints. 'Though I live with Boris,
I never would call him familiar names.
In Russia, you know, we respect one who is
Older than us' (the shadow slows) 'and
Boris is older. But let us continue!
He will not join in, yet he can understand.'

Ykaterina Vladimirovna,
Married in church, you cough into dawn
As Boris smokes, to disappear
Upon patrol. You list new poets,
Sleep late; miss breakfast; line your eyes
Immaculate blue, the Virgin's tones,
Translate; count glasses. Each hot day
Inside your head in gold, domed Russia,
You knock, for somewhere safe to stay.

'Now we go to the British cemetery'

If you are buried by the busy road
You will be washed by Archangel's foul air.
All the branches pulped and shredded there
Shed over a bleached verge their final load
Past sky-blue railings round the Russian tombs
The wild grass gives up its hidden plumes

To rain, to silence. Russia grows few flowers
By wooden shacks and concrete balconies.
Red clover here sweeps taller than my knees
Past burning blue of vetch the nettle towers,
Till I walk, stumbling on the boggy ground
Where in your broken ranks you stand around

Young sailors, mostly, drowned in civil war
We had forgotten. Did you understand?
Or from the last, most famous war, to land
Brought with charred numbers, quieter than before.
Glow, daisies. Are you lucky? Could you still
Live by the silent birches of Chernobyl?

You would have grasped at that before you fell.
Anything flashed better than to go.
Survival is the duty which we know
Too late; the green fence, where the lilac spills
Scrawny, unseen. Beyond the crushed grass, our
Accustomed breath is tasted like a kiss,
On the broad pavement, where the live air's sour.

On the Northern Line

It begins with Kh. Cyrillic snarls syllables.
I thought it might be a second valley, white
With whizzing midges, where the bellflower falls
Evening purple and the dragonflies
Hum flying violet, till the children bring
Woolled puppies, tall bikes, where the long hay lies.

A cage of cables rears above our heads.
Sewage is running milky through the stream.
(Someone set amber lilies in the beds
Of heaped sand on the platform.) By the shed
A diesel engine glints. Into its cab
The driver clambers, clasping something red.

Carnations – no, the stopper on a can,
Oil, or water, something he must need.
There does not seem much more here for a man:
Gravel, a scrapyard, where the cabs lie piled.
He has his bundled food, his brilliant can,
Though I, yet hopeful, watched for something wild.

I glance up to his face. Why is he smiling,
Climbing to work, under a drowning sky?
His cheek is browner than the sand's dust, whirling
Up from his town. His train, the unlocked power,
Waits for him. As scarlet signals die,
He clangs the door. I cannot see the flower.

1829

In the year 1829, when Mozart had been dead for over 30 years, his wife Constanza was still alive, alert – though a little frail – and living quietly in Salzburg. There she was visited by an English couple, the Novellos, with whom she talked at length.

In the poem, the first and final sections are spoken by Mozart, the second by Constanza. From death and life, they pursue their argument with a certain Viennese lady, Fräulein von Greiner, whose memoirs had been ecstatic about Mozart's music, but less than complimentary about Mozart himself. They remember others: their two surviving children, Carl and Franz, Puchberg, Mozart's most generous creditor, and Sussmaier, his last pupil.

Many of the poem's details are history. Thanks to the creditors' inventory, we know the exact contents of Mozart's apartment, down to the six 'ordinary glasses' left in his study.

I

In my new room, between Vienna and Virgo,
The air, like good coffee, tastes fragrant and black.
In shifting starlight I read a page
By Fräulein von Greiner. A half-life ago
She turned her fine nose and her classical gaze
On her father's stiff salon, for which I played.
She murmurs, 'He was the most ordinary soul,
Who preferred, to our learning, the silliest joke.
He jumped on a chair, then miaowed, like a cat!'

'Will she still pay you?' my young wife cried,
Although I had sung her the Fräulein's shock,
The lilting cry from the throat of a cat.
Disturbed, she woke, loud morning near;
Pupils hummed luminous and black
Moon's answers tugged warm seas to fold.
No work is ever finished here,
The rush of space whirls each hot globe.
Dear gallop's heart, can she be old?

II

I lean my stick against the bed
As straight and brittle as my bones.
The green quilt's watered pattern glows
Like the fine coat he last had made.
Today, the English couple came
Who worship him. The kind wife wept,
She hugged me; but her husband stepped
Back shrewdly; watched me seek his name.

He saw how small – and faint – it blew,
That light from forty years ago.
I also loved the next man who
Paid bills, made notes, slept quiet by me.
But they asked of that hard, first end.
I told my story, smoothly learned.

'The stranger wore the long still face
A doctor makes. He said, "Someone
Most dear has died. Her Requiem
Has been commissioned, at your price.
Your patron's name must not be known."'
Strange terms! I almost laughed at them.

'As we climbed on the Prague post-coach'
(I had left Franz, turned four weeks old)
'A hand dragged on my heavy cloak.
"It is not ready." No reproach.
"It shall be done, when I return."
The grave man nodded, barely spoke.

They met again; I was away,
With the children, in the storm-tossed park.
Skies battered with rain. He sat alone.
I made him drive with me next day.
He said the work was not for her,
The strange, dead girl. It was his own.'

How could I know that she was young?
When that hand clutched, my body shook
In the child's last shudder. It is all true.
How desperate we were then, how young.
I hid beneath the sodden sheets
In his heat's ruin; would die too.

The last bill for his sea-green coat
Lay with the rest. I wept again
To see the wreck of our affairs.
The papers shone in glare of snow.
Once he was gone, our money grew.
The dead cannot insult gilt chairs.

When I had woken, weighed and wrung
By Puchberg's loans; four children gone;
He would turn, to speak the silly
Warming names which licked rough tongues.
He drowned; I breathe. High in this room's
Neat wastes, who laughs? who aches for me?

That clever Fräulein and her guests,
Even the kindly English, want
Something grander than the sun
Of ordinary happiness.
It only dazzles them when glanced
Down from its flying, frozen, done

Fräulein von Greiner, cats may sing.
I sing the last notes that he wrote.
I hear him walk to that fresh dark
Slow as my stick taps, note by note.

III

That my name is strange as a star:

that she forgets my voice, my hands

that she marries again,

                      this is death, as life makes it.

The water is streaming along the small road
the carthorse foal, his awkward head
spiked with spring's mud, rushes up to the coach.
Carl points to him, cries.

I could set that; any note. I caught
Constanza's raw cries as she struggled with Carl.

She could not sing high, as her sisters could,
the two mad birds at the top of the voice.
I would have had one. To have high notes for ever –

but no, we live on the middle road
the coach slowing and rocking, the carthorse foal
spinning away and Carl's thin voice singing.

She left me too, she went away
to those costly cures – what did Puchberg say?
'Is she a fish?' – and I laughed, and saw
Constanza at Baden, with half-closed eyes
in the murky expensive baths,
floating, the heavy child hung light
as the milk stars whirl, in her private dark
she swims, and her arms are slender and bare,
stronger than mine. There she floats, and smiles.

If stars asked questions, they would say
'Was it hard?' It burned the mind.
As you would know, Constanza, with
Your cracking voice, as they would know
Ringed with the iris of their fires.

Something comes to hold us back.
It drags and jars the carriage wheels.
I never loved those small dark rooms –
Black stove, dull glassware, shut from day –
In which we lived. To move's to live.
The roofs, the small fields fall away.

Your sister, Sophie, told the truth.
'The open score lay on the bed.
He twitched his mouth to show Sussmaier
The drum's pulse: the last sound he made.'

He set it wrong; I saw he would,
I could not teach him anything.
The Masons cleared the choking bills.
How smooth things ran, like Sussmaier's drums!
Listen, you fool: there is a start:
The jolt of heart, the sudden kiss,
As first sun beats to rake the skin.

Carl, whose kindly crooked face
Could never take one lesson in
Has somehow made a bookkeeper.
She taught Franz all my songs, then hoped
To coax him to a prodigy.
His swift career has veered, instead,
Into a Polish Countess's bed.

They are my children. They are brave,
Powerful as these icy lights.
She, straight-backed on her green bed
Is silence in its straightest flight.

What planet now wears my old coat
Washed by the rain, as fine as grass?
What lost suns from the shadows' height
Throb radiance through my cheap glass?

Frost

How slowly it grows.
Ground still gives to the foot.
But the mole tastes the cold
That's to come round the root.

His mounds sweep in circles
Fresh darkness gripped white.
'Ninety-nine –' counts the child
Then coughs through the night.

The blood slows. Sight narrows
To white tunnels. Raw
In his sudden wet passage
The mole smells the thaw.